YOUR MONEY
YOUR CHOICE

A Thought Provoking Guide To Help Jump Start

Your Financial Journey!

CHIVON OBIRI-MAINOO

Copyrighted Material

ISBN-13:978-1542815796
ISBN-10: 1542815797

Visit the website:
www.chivonmotivates.com

Contents

Let's Meet

From a young age, I learned how the lack of money management can affect people's lives. This became my reality when after graduating from college with over $25,000 in student loan debt and a new car  note, I realized to be successful with my finances I had to do the opposite of what everyone around me was doing; borrowing to spend. With this mindset, I adopted the "cash only" approach system.

Simply explained, if I didn't have the cash to pay for it now, I wouldn't buy it now. Being newly married and having a combined debt load of over $100,000, I took the same discipline from being a former collegiate athlete and purposed to pay it off and be debt free within two years and I did exactly that. I realized that to amass wealth and change family legacies, one has to be diligent and disciplined to live their greatest life financially.

We all have choices in what we do with money. I made the decision to go against the norms to change my financial future and I hope you will be inspired to do the same.

Introduction

Ever felt guilty about your financial state? Like you want to make changes in your finances, but time after time, you make the same mistakes? Or do you have money, but don't make the best choices? We have the choice to change our situation if it is not working to our benefit.

I want to congratulate you on taking a step to improve your financial situation! This guide was created to break down the overwhelming feeling of helplessness when you sit down to analyze your finances and the deep knowledge that the picture on the canvas isn't a good one. If you don't like sitting down and pulling out all of your documents at one time to figure out your financial situation, don't worry! This guide is just for you!

Just take fifteen minutes every day for the next thirty days to answer simple questions. Questions which will give you clarity on your thought process about finances and a closer reality about your current financial state. I believe by the end of guide you will want to take actionable steps to change your financial future.

Financial Attitude

For the next eight days, we will focus on how you view money. Think deeply and answer honestly. The goal in this section is to get you to understand why you view money the way you do. Is it genetics or something else? Some of the questions may seem redundant, but it is all aimed at getting you to analyze your situation from different vantage points.

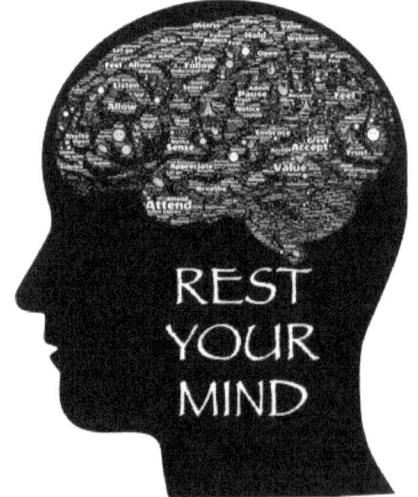

Knowledge Base

A study by the University of Washington and Claremont McKenna College collaboration concluded that heredity or genetics plays a key role in our attitudes towards money. They found out that genetics accounts for one-third, on average, and as much as 45 percent of investor behavior. Other factors previously studied, such as age, gender, education, wealth and home ownership, when combined explain only 5 to 10 percent of investor behavior.

Understanding this phenomenon is essential to your success. The following are some tips on how to approach change.

Understand your attitude towards money. Once you understand how you view and relate to money, finding ways to cut out the bad behavior is easier as opposed to fighting yourself to be something that you are inherently not.

Appreciate the fact that you are how you are, but be prepared to listen to people who are unlike you in order to learn how to wean yourself from the bad habits. Remember to take small steps at a time. Drastic changes might cause frustration and demoralize you in your quest. Start slow and congratulate yourself on the smallest of accomplishments.

Soon you will find that these bad habits are becoming easier to avoid thereby increasing the chances of changing your financial legacy for the better.

THINK ABOUT IT

Day 1: *"Saving money isn't about being able to buy bigger and better things. It's about being prepared to take care of your family."* — **Dave Ramsey**

What inspires you to obtain money? (Motivation is the drive to do something)

Day 2: *"People get blinded by money; money with no sense of guidance is the same as being poor."* — **David Katz**

Did you come from a humble or affluent background? How do you think this shaped your perception of money?

Day 3: *"Money is only a tool. It will take you wherever you wish, but it will not replace you as the driver."* — **Ayn Rand**

Who are the top three individuals that influenced your financial decision-making? What have they taught you?

Day 4: *"You do pay a price for your Financial Freedom, but it is far lesser than what you pay for a Lifetime of Slavery." —* **Manoj Arora**

Are you happy that these individuals influenced your life financially? Are/were they living the lifestyle you want?

Day 5: *"Do not value money for any more nor any less than its worth; it is a good servant but a bad master."* — Alexandre Dummas Fils

Are others' perceptions of your financial situation important to you? Why or Why Not?

Day 6: *"Not he who has much is rich, but he who gives much."* — Erich Fromm

Whether you're earning the income that you hope for or not, what are some factors preventing you from being the best you can be financially?

Day 7: *"The first step into becoming financially successful is to stop taking financial advice from your broke family members and friends."* — **Chivon Obiri-Mainoo**

Do you have anyone in your life right now, a spouse, relative, or friend that would impact your financial progress? How?

Day 8: *"Rich people stay rich by living like they're broke. Broke people stay broke by living like they're rich."* — **Bill Murray**

If you had all the money you needed, what would you do with it?

Congratulations on completing the first eight days aimed at shedding some insight on your financial attitude.

Helpful Tips

❖ If you have individuals in your life that are not in a good financial position, it is imperative that you stop taking financial advice from them. This is one of the biggest factors that prevent us from being successful because we are not taking advice from financially literate people.

❖ If you have individuals who are frequently asking you for money or always in crises and you're always helping them out, you really need to re-evaluate if you are helping or enabling these individuals. You might think you are helping them, but you may be impeding their ability to be financially independent especially if they have bad financial behaviors.

Also, you're hurting yourself, especially if you are not in the financial position to do so. This is hindering your ability to achieve financial freedom and then be in the position to help others who may really need help as opposed to those that ask for help all the time without trying to help themselves.

<u>Budgeting</u>

Imagine getting into your car and needing to go to a specific address (for example, 300 Main Street, Manhattan, NY). If you were to put into your GPS, simply Manhattan, NY will it take you to 300 Main Street? No! Why is this? It's because you weren't specific in telling  the GPS where you needed to go. The same thing applies with our money. Intentional spending (also known as budgeting) is the key to winning with money. That is why it's imperative for you to establish the difference between wants and needs.

The next seven days will assist you in knowing where you stand when it comes to budgeting. Answer the questions honestly and thoroughly to get the most out of this exercise.

Day 9: *"It's not an issue of Wants vs. Needs. It's an issue of Wants vs. Priorities."* — **Unknown Author**

What is the difference between a want versus a need?

Knowledge Base

A need is something that is essential to your survival. These are:

- ❖ Food
- ❖ Utilities
- ❖ Transportation (basic)
- ❖ Water
- ❖ Clothes (basic)
- ❖ Shelter

A want is something that is not essential for survival, but you would like to have such as:

- ❖ Designer Clothes
- ❖ Cable Television
- ❖ Smart Cell Phone
- ❖ Vacations
- ❖ Eating out

THINK ABOUT IT

Day 10: *"Ask yourself if what you're buying is a need or a want. There's a big difference."* — **Unknown Author**

Do you believe the majority of your income goes towards wants or needs? Why?

Day 11: *"Live below your means and within your needs."* — Suzie Orman

Do you live below, at or above your means?

Knowledge Base

Living beyond your means is spending more than you have. Put another way, spending more on wants than on needs.

Living within your means is when you spend only the amount of money you have. You may use credit occasionally and really don't have a savings account because you spend all you have each month.

Living beneath your means is when you do not spend all your money all the time. You have found a perfect balance between wants and needs. You have surplus funds and can easily participate in extra-curricular activities.

THINK ABOUT IT

Day 12: *"A budget is telling your money where to go instead of wondering where it went."* — **Dave Ramsey**

Do you complete a monthly budget at the beginning of each month? Why or Why not?

Day 13: *"My problem lies in reconciling my gross habits with my net income."* — Errol Flynn

What is your estimated net (after taxes) take home pay weekly, bi-weekly, or monthly?

Day 14: *"Don't tell me where your priorities are. Show me where you spend your money and I'll tell you what they are."* — **James W. Frick**

What is the estimated monthly amount you spend on needs? (Rent/mortgage, utilities, food, basic clothing and transportation)

Day 15: *"It's not your salary that makes you rich; it's your spending habits."* — **Charles A. Jaffe**

What is the estimated weekly amount you spend eating out? This includes (coffee purchases, lunches, and dinner). If you don't know these amounts start to keep track by keeping all your receipts and writing it down.

Let's Learn How to Budget

Congratulations on getting through the last seven days. Now that you have a clearer picture of your income and expenses, let's give you some tools on how to successfully start the budgeting process.

1) Every month before the month begins, set a day and time that you will sit down and work on your monthly budget for thirty minutes (ex: I will devote 30 minutes on March 30, 2017 to work on my budget)

2) If you are married, it is vital that you get your spouse involved. When you are not on the same page in changing your financial future, it will be difficult to have success.

3) Every week you will devote fifteen minutes to reconciling your checkbook. Whether this is on excel, or an accounting software such as Microsoft Money or QuickBooks, or manually.

4) For small business owners, deductr.com is a new platform that automates everything for you to track your income, expenses, mileage and you won't miss tax deductions that you

should be getting. No more carrying around and filing your receipts. Just take a picture and assign a category and that's it. When it's time to file taxes, you can just print a report for your accountant. It's definitely worth the cost ($199/year or $19.95/month). Individuals can use this as well.

5) When you are creating a budget, make sure that you are allocating every dollar to a category. This is called a zero based budget because all dollars will be spent. You should make it a habit to always pay yourself first before you pay anyone else. This is a percentage of your net income. This amount should be anywhere from 5%-10%. Then, before you handle anything else you should cover the following:

❖ Food

❖ Shelter (Rent or Mortgage)

❖ Clothing

❖ Basic Transportation

❖ Utilities

6) After the above is expensed, you can start allocating your dollars to your other categories.

(On the next page you can refer to the desired allocations, I used the financial guru Dave Ramsey's because his percentages are more on the conservative side for net take home pay).

Financial Guru Dave Ramsey Percentage Guidelines

Category	Percentage of Overall Spending
Housing	25%-35%
Utilities	5%-10%
Transportation	10%-15%
Healthcare	5%-10%
Food	5%-15%
Investments/Savings	5%-10%
Debt Payments	5%-10%
Charitable Giving	5%-15%
Entertainment/Recreation	5%-9%
Misc. Personal	2%-7%

Zero Based Budget

Monthly Take Home Pay	$ 1,000.00
Pay yourself	$100
Balance	**$900**

Then take care of the following:

Rent/Mortgage	$300
Food	$100
Utilities	$50
Car Expenses	$150
Clothing	$30

Then proceed to other categories:

Debt	$50
Entertaiment	$30
Toiletries	$20
Gym Membership	$30
Investments	$50
Kid Activities	$45
Other	$45
Total	**$0**

<u>Debt</u>

Debt is allowing another to have claim against you. It presumes upon the future because we believe that future conditions will allow us to repay that debt. It's what prevents us from reaching our financial goals and being able to save accordingly.

For the next six days, we will focus on broadening our understanding of debt and how to recognize it as a hindrance to our financial well-being.

Knowledge Base

No one is immune to the detrimental effects of debt. Debt tends to be often, more than just money. Knowing you owe someone money can lead to a barrage of other emotional and psychological issues.

Did you know that the average American has $15,950 in credit card debt, and 39% of Americans carry credit card debt month to month? This is per a study conducted by CreditCards.com.

Add college students who on an average graduate with about $40,000 of student loans. Other loans such as mortgages, medical debt and other financial obligations makes it a safe bet that a majority of Americans carry some sort of debt!

According to CNBC the average monthly car payments has gone over the $500 mark and the average car term has gone up to 68 months (almost 6 years).

THINK ABOUT IT

Day 16: *"Some debts are fun when you are acquiring them, but none are fun when you set about retiring them."* — **Ogden Nash**

What is your estimated debt load? This may include student loans, car loans, credit cards, home equity loans, business loans, unpaid taxes, or any collection bills. Good idea to look up your credit report.

You can request your free credit report once a year from all three credit bureaus:

- ❖ Experian
- ❖ Transunion
- ❖ Equifax

Day 17: *"The art is not making money, but in keeping it."* — **Proverb**

Do you believe having debt is the way of life? Why or Why not?

Day 18: *"The only man who sticks closer to you in adversity than a friend is a creditor."*— Unknown Author

Are you stressed out by your current debt load which may be manifested by the never ending calls from bill collectors? How does this manifest itself?

Day 19: *"I would rather go to bed without dinner than rise in debt."* — **Benjamin Franklin**

If buying a major item, do you equate affordability with the ability to make monthly payments?

Day 20: *"Don't buy things you can't afford with money you don't have to impress people you don't like!"*— **Dave Ramsey**

If you do not have the cash to buy an item, do you buy it anyway? Why or why not?

Day 21: *"Cash is King, and queen, and prince, and princess, and duke and duchess, and and and…."*— **Unknown Author**

Are most of your purchases made with cash or debit/credit cards? Why or why not?

Helpful Tips

❖ If debt is overwhelming you and you want to get out of it, the first thing you must do is <u>STOP BORROWING.</u>

❖ When you feel the urge to want to buy an item that you don't have the cash to pay for, wait and think about it for <u>24 hours</u>. This will slow down your emotional feelings (aka impulse buying) that you are having at the moment.

❖ <u>Cut</u> up all your credit cards and only keep one. Why do I say this? If you're in credit card debt it proves you do not have the discipline to pay off the card every month or current circumstances do not allow you to pay it off.

❖ <u>Don't worry</u> about credit score right now because you have a spending issue which is costing you more interest and potential fees.

❖ If you have overdraft fees combined with your debt, move to a cash system. Many times we think we are saving more by using a debit credit card, but studies by Dun & Bradstreet found that people spend <u>12-18% more</u> using cards than cash.

- ❖ Many times people say they don't want to carry around cash because it's not safe. This is just ridiculous. No one is telling you to carry around $1,000, but if you need $200 for groceries, just take out the $200 and go grocery shopping.

- ❖ If you often purchase items without having the funds to cover, get an accountability partner who you can run these purchases by before you pull the trigger. Please pick an individual who is financially responsible and won't aid in unproductive behavior.

- ❖ You must gain power over purchases. Remember, advertisers spend billions of dollars trying to get your dollars. They do not want you to have financial freedom.

- ❖ Wealthy people ask how much? Broke people ask how much the monthly payments are. Just because you think you can afford monthly payments doesn't mean you are able to afford that item. Example, if you make $30,000 a year and buy a $15,000 car because you think you can afford the monthly payments, in actuality you can't afford that car. It is an asset worth half your annual income that is going down in value...aka depreciating.

❖ Never, Never, Never cosign for anyone unless you are willing to pay the bill which is a high probability. If the bank doesn't trust the person enough to give the loan to the person without you, why would you take on this responsibility?

❖ Parents' student loan debt is rising. Yes, our children are 18 which mean that they are legal adults, however, you would never let them go and purchase a $60,000 luxury vehicle. Why? Because you know they can't afford it. Well, it's the same logic with college education. Just because you hear the word education doesn't mean the same financial principles do not apply. Education is important, don't get me wrong, but we live in an age where we have access to information at our finger tips.

Paying thousands to go somewhere that one can't afford when there are so many alternative options such as a two year school and then transferring over to a four your school. Think about going to an in state versus a private university. Did you know that if you go to an out of state school you pay thousands more? Also, being a commuter instead of living on campus will cut costs dramatically.

Student loan debt is one of the causes that is putting our young people into financial bondage. They come out of school trying to dig themselves out of this debt, in addition to trying to find meaningful employment to cover their expenses. Make sure you are running the numbers when it comes to your child's college decisions.

Savings

More often than not, our response to savings is
that we do not have enough money
to save; however, it is always amazing how we find money to do that
thing that we always want to do. If
we prioritize savings, we will find
the money to do so. For the next
five days, we will dig deeper into savings and how
it can change our finances for the better.

Knowledge Base

❖ Did you know, according to a study conducted by the Washington Post, 46% of Americans do not have enough cash on hand to handle a $400 emergency without going to family members and friends? This means that individuals live life on the assumption that someone is always going to bail them out when they get into a bind.

❖ Another amazing discovery by CNN Money stated that 64% of Americans do not have enough cash on hand to handle a $1,000 emergency. Some women spend that alone on hair appointments, clothes, shoes, and accessories, and for some men, it may be power tools or the latest computer gadgets or gaming systems.

❖ Nearly half of American households are one emergency away from financial disaster according to the Huffington Post. This means that if one is not able to bring in a paycheck, it can have detrimental effects on the family. That's why it's more important than ever to take a step in getting one's finances in order.

❖ The average household spends $2,482 a year on entertainment according to simple dollar.com. Now if we really break this down, some other items are being put into this category. Imagine if this amount was cut in half, $1,241 this could be applied to savings. Therefore, even though we claim extremely tight budgets and many are living paycheck to paycheck; if we really analyze our spending, we can find ways to save money. We just need to prioritize this desire.

THINK ABOUT IT

Day 22: *"Save Money and Money will save you."* — **Unknown Author**

How much are you saving weekly or monthly?

Day 23: *"There's always something coming in a few months that will cost money. So be prepared!* — **Unknown Author**

Do you have enough cash on hand to cover a $1,000 emergency? Have you had any emergencies in the past that you didn't have the money to cover?

Day 24: *"You can borrow money for College. But you can't borrow for Retirement."* — Unknown Author

Are you saving towards retirement, a college education, or something else?

Helpful Tips

❖ Get a $1,000 emergency fund in place if you don't already have one. I would suggest 3-6 months of your income (more on the 6 month side) if you can afford it. This will keep you from borrowing and you will find that unexpected events, aka, emergencies, will cause less stress.

❖ If you feel you can't afford to immediately save $1,000, are there expenses that you can cut (for example, cable or eating out) or are you able to bring in more income?

❖ If you feel that $1,000 is out of your savings range, start with $500 and then work your way up to $1,000.

❖ Anytime you have to use your emergency fund make sure you are always replenishing it to the original level.

❖ Automation is a great way to start saving. What is automation? Before you even see the money, set up with your bank to have a certain amount of money withdrawn automatically on a particular day of the month into another account or investment. I suggest doing this between days

1 to 5 so you're not tempted to use the funds for other things.

❖ Money Market accounts are great accounts to have an emergency fund in because it offers slightly higher interest rates than regular savings accounts and it has check writing privileges. Try not to have this at the same bank that you have your regular checking or savings account because you will be less tempted to use the funds.

❖ If you are not saving for retirement, the time is now. You can open a Roth IRA for as little as $50/month. The great thing about a Roth IRA investment is that when you retire, your withdrawals are tax free, since you are contributing with after tax dollars. Also, if you need to, you're able to withdraw any amount you contributed, tax free.

❖ If you have college bound children, investing now for this venture is essential. Half a loaf of bread is better than nothing thus even the smallest of investments could go a long way in your future plan. Below are some plans worth looking into:

- Coverdell Education Saving Account- $2,000 maximum contribution per year.

- 529 Plan- is an education plan operated by the state to help families save. There is no annual contribution limits with this plan.

- The Fidelity's U-Fund has a gifting option where you can send family members and friends a link or they can write a check to contribute to your child's education fund.

❖ Many of these plans you can contribute as little as $25-$50/month.

❖ When it comes to activities that you want to do, for instance going on a vacation in the summer time, open a separate account or get an envelope and label it "The Vacation Fund" and figure out how much you need. If this amount is $500 and it's five months away, you are going to add a line item to your monthly budget called "vacation" for the amount of $100 ($500/5). If you use this concept for other events that take place, you will find that you won't be robbing Peter to pay Paul or borrowing to cover them (example on next page).

Monthly Take Home Pay	$ 1,000
Pay yourself	$100
Balance	$900

Then take care of the following:

Rent/Mortgage	$300
Food	$100
Utilities	$100
Car Expenses (can include car note, insurance, gas)	$300
Vacation Fund	**$100**

Total	**$0**

Day 25: *"Intention without action is an insult to those who expect the best from you."* — **Andy Andrews**

If you don't have an emergency fund established or you are not saving per the principles outlined in the knowledge base section above, what steps are you going to take to implement this into your finances?

Day 26: *"You cannot change your destination overnight, but you can change your direction overnight."* — **Jim Rohn**

Today is about goal setting. How quickly will you get this $1,000 emergency fund established (month?). For those who are in a better finances position, write down how quickly you can get your 3 to 6 months fund established. This would be 3 to 6 months of your net take home pay.

<u>Insurance</u>

If you have others depending on you, and something was to happen to you today and you could no longer provide that support, how certain are you in the knowledge that your dependents will be secure?

It is often sad to hear a family having to scramble for money to bury their loved one or there isn't any financial investment left behind for surviving dependents when a life insurance policy could have been purchased for less than $50 a month depending on health and age.

It's also important to consider how your income would be replaced if you became disabled either temporarily or permanently and unable to work.

Insurance is instrumental in achieving a healthy financial legacy. For the next two days we will focus on the important aspects of this formidable topic.

Knowledge Base

The following sobering stats are from the Business Insider:

❖ 1 in 3 Americans coming into the workforce will become disabled at some point in their career.

❖ Close to 90% of disabilities are not covered by workers compensation because even though it removes a person from the workforce, they aren't specifically work related.

❖ Short term disability which would be used if you were out of work for several weeks or months pays you anywhere from 50-70% of your salary which usually last 3-6 months.

❖ Long term disability has an average duration of 2.5 years and pays you 40-65% of your salary.

THINK ABOUT IT

Day 27: *"If a child, a spouse, a life partner, or a parent depends on you and your income, you need life insurance".* — **Suze Orman**

Do you have a life insurance policy that is at least 10 times your annual salary? If yes, is this held with your current employer? If no, why not? List all policies with amounts and companies it's held with.

Day 28: *"Do something today that your future self will thank you for."* — **Unknown Author**

Do you have short-term and long-term disability insurance in case you weren't able to work in the event of a disability? If no, why not?

Helpful Tips

❖ A Term Insurance policy is going to be cost effective for most individuals rather than a Whole Life policy. Agents will try to sell you on whole life because it is permanent and has a cash value component, but it's very expensive. Many individuals do not know that you lose this cash value component upon death and it has an insignificant rate of return. Unless you have substantial assets where you would work with a financial planner who is using this as a part of your estate planning, Whole Life policy is not suggested.

❖ If you do not have a Term Life policy outside your employer, it is suggested that you do so because if you ever leave that employer, that policy doesn't go with you. Also, most employer sponsored policies go up only to a certain amount based on your annual salary.

❖ Always get a life insurance policy 10 to 12 times your annual income. If you make $30,000/year you're looking at a policy of $300,000 to $360,000.

❖ Most employers offer short term disability insurance and some offer long term as well. Even though it is cheaper, it may not offer the most comprehensive plan, but always opt in for these plans. It is suggested to look at plans outside your employer, but this can be expensive so you may be better off building up that emergency fund.

❖ For self-employed individuals, it is strongly recommended that you look into getting a policy even if it may be a little expensive. There isn't an outside employer who is going to cover you.

❖ www.zanderinsurance.com is a company that you can call and they will assist in locating the best life insurance/disability insurance quotes from different companies.

Time of Reflection

The last two days will be a time of reflection and contemplation. A time to analyze all you've learnt and the people to surround yourself with to best assist you in attaining financial independence.

Day 29: *"Planning is bringing the future into the present, so that you can do something about it now."* — **Alain Lakein**

Now that you have been through this journey, how would you assess your current financial situation? Do you feel better or worse? Why?

Day 30: *"You are the root of your financial success or failure. If you work on the roots, the fruits will take care of themselves."—* **Unknown Author**

You made it! Write down three people that you believe can hold you accountable when making financial decisions. These are individuals who are good with money. If you are married, you are holding each other accountable. If you are not in agreement with your spouse about money, start to write down what you think you need to do for the both of you to get on the same page. You may need to seek counseling.

So Now What?

You didn't come this far to give up. There are a few considerations right now to be conscious of. Some of you will want to reach out immediately for that professional support and guidance and if so, that's great because you realize you need help and don't want to waste any more time. Some of you are grateful for the self-reflection, but still may not see the urgency of your situation and that is understandable. Whatever category you fall in, I hope you know that people like me exist to help you achieve your financial goals. We serve as instruments to guide and motivate you to get to that level that you can sit back and say, "future, bring it on, because I am ready and boy, it sure feels good!"

Contact Me

You can check out my website for speaking, workshops and personal financial coaching at:

Website: chivonmotivates.com
Facebook: Chivon Obiri-Mainoo
Instagram: ChivonObiriMainoo